Interior Design
COLORING BOOK
for Adults

THIS BOOK
BELONGS TO:

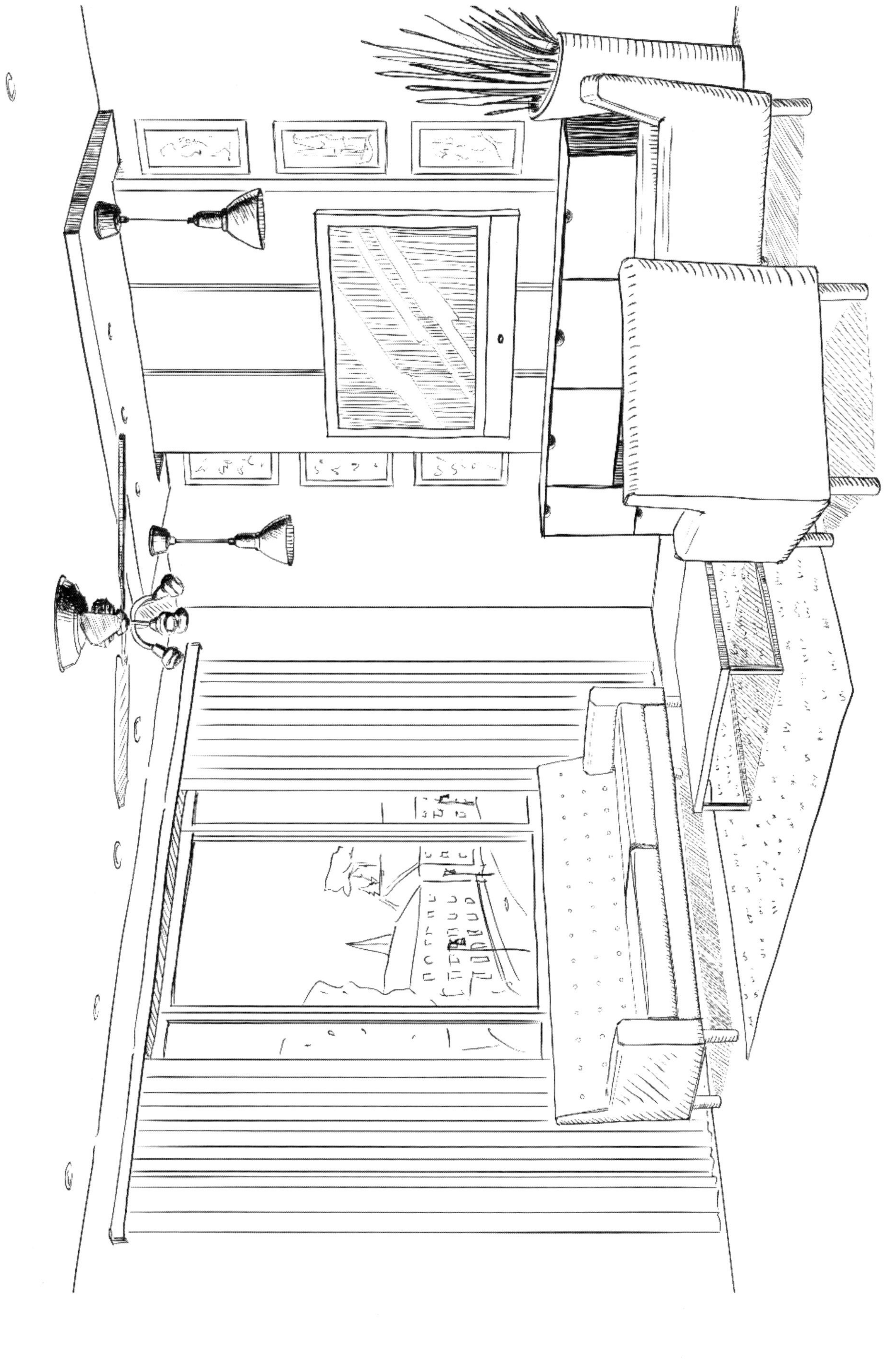

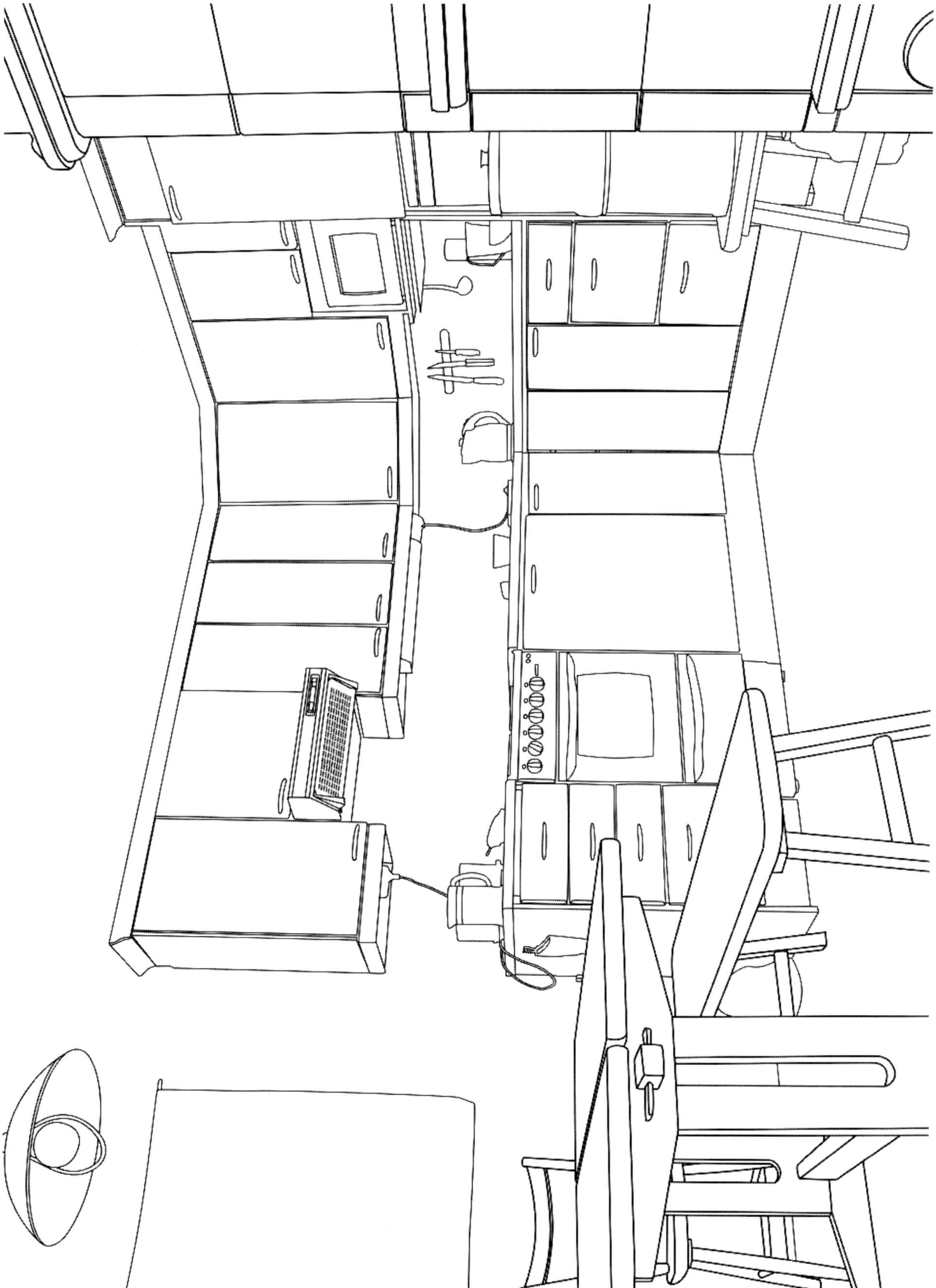

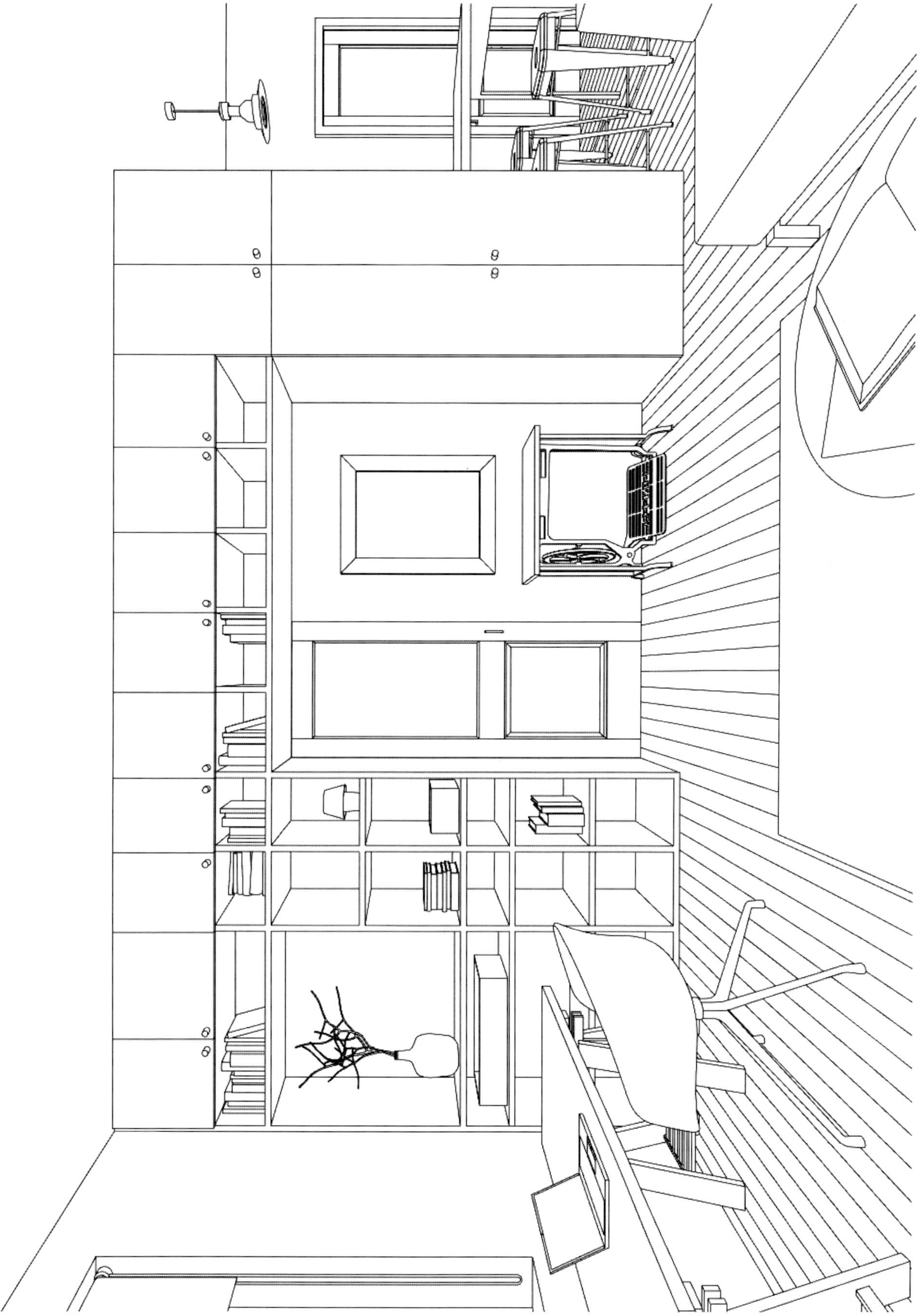

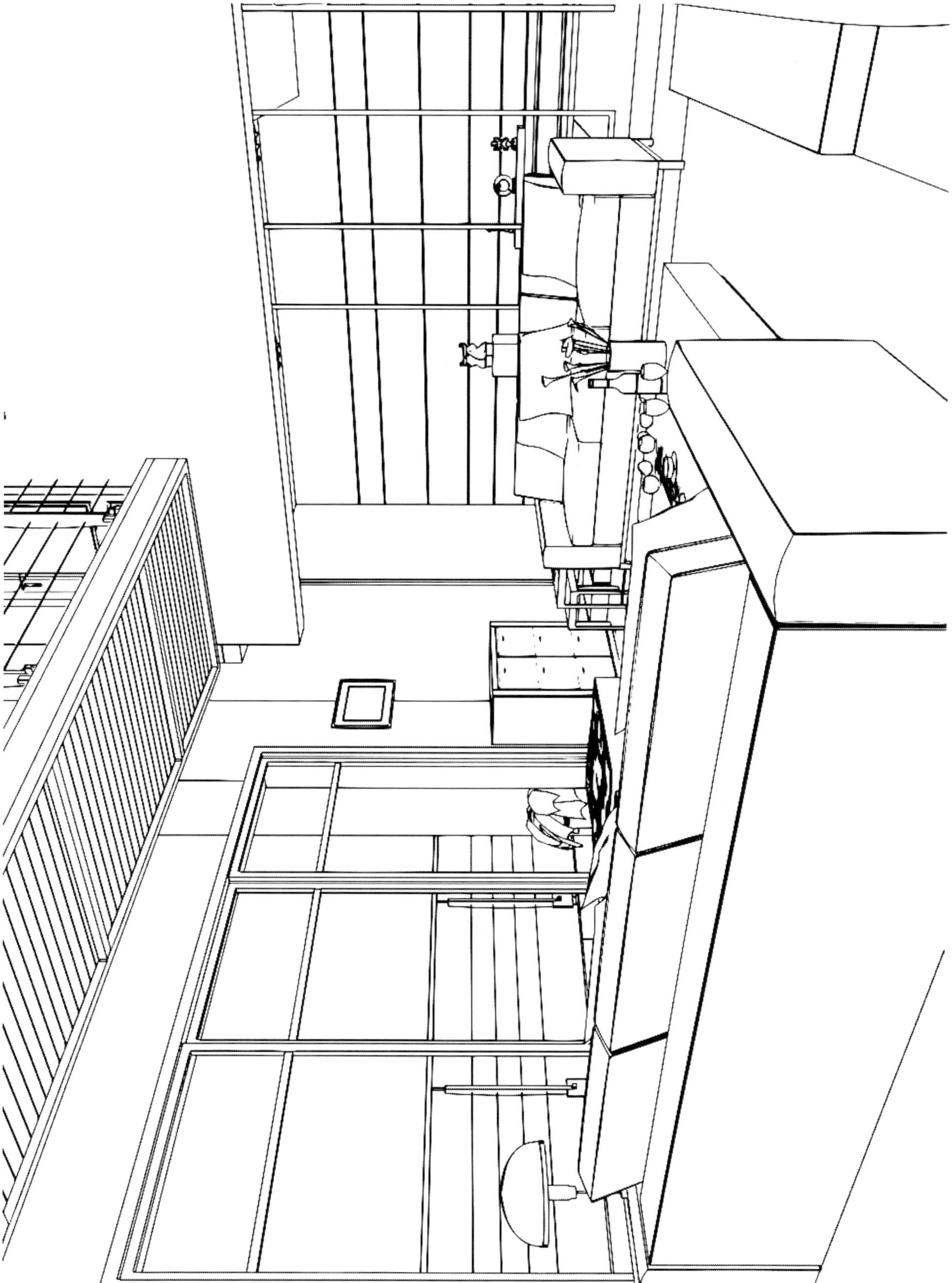

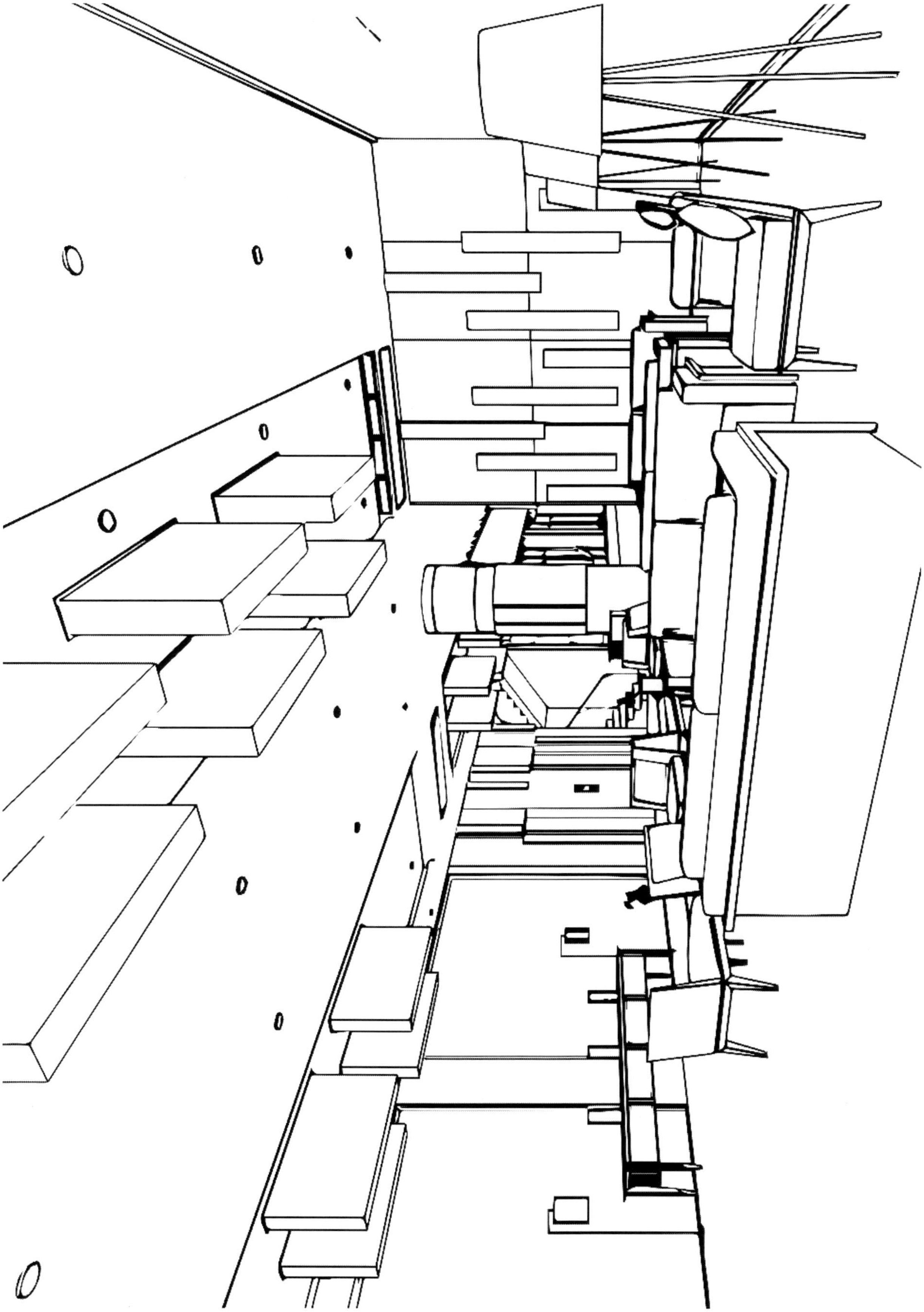

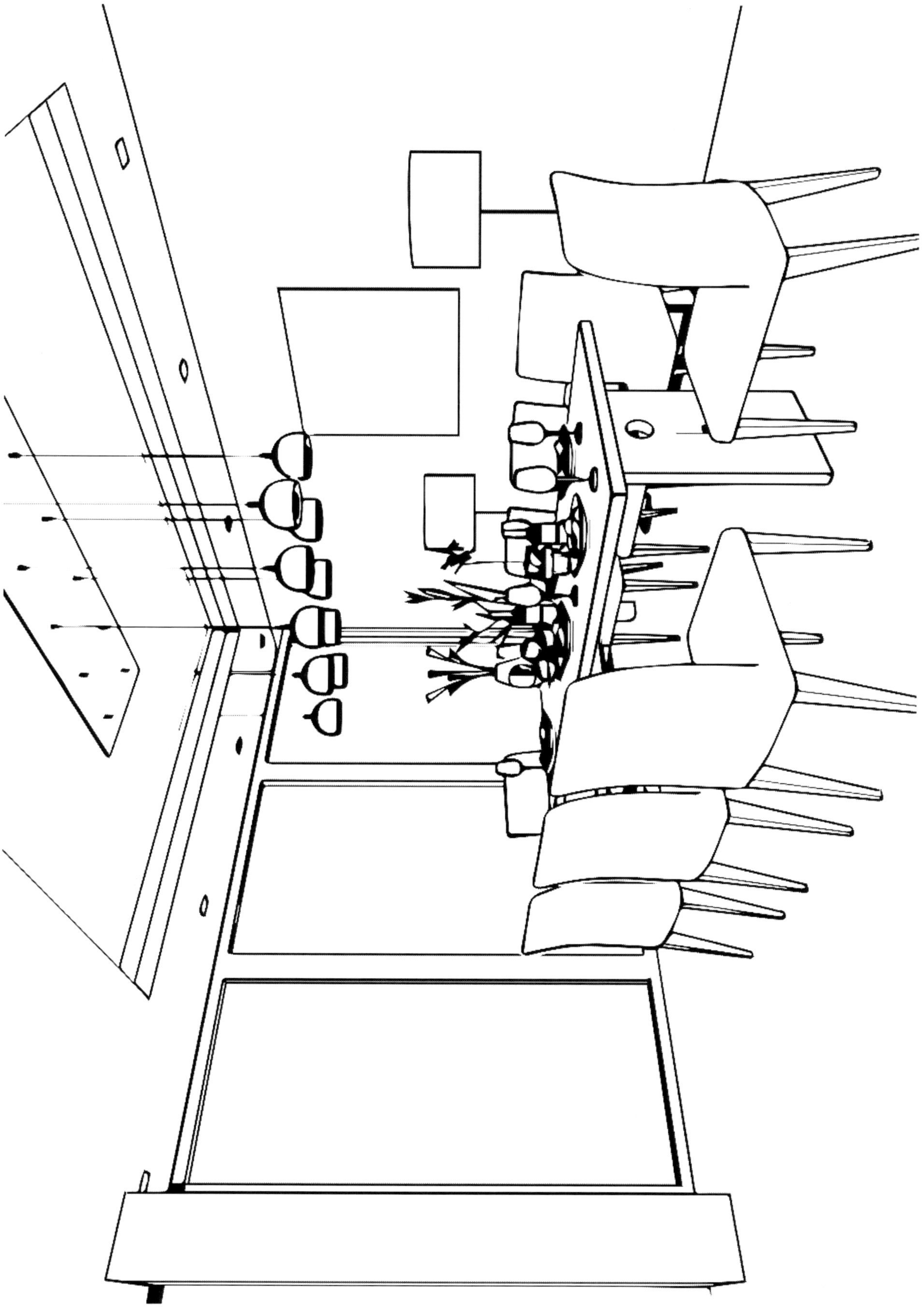

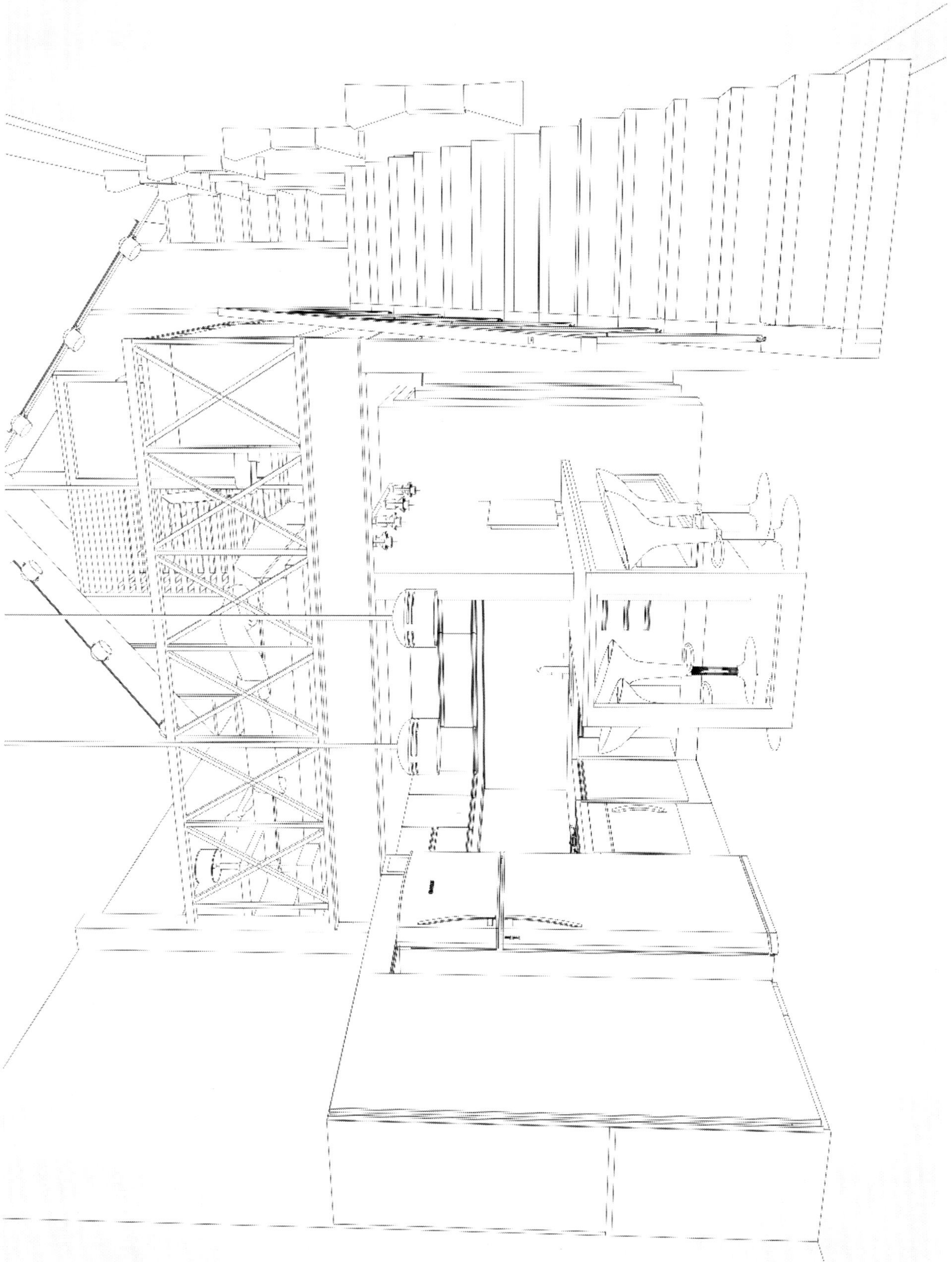

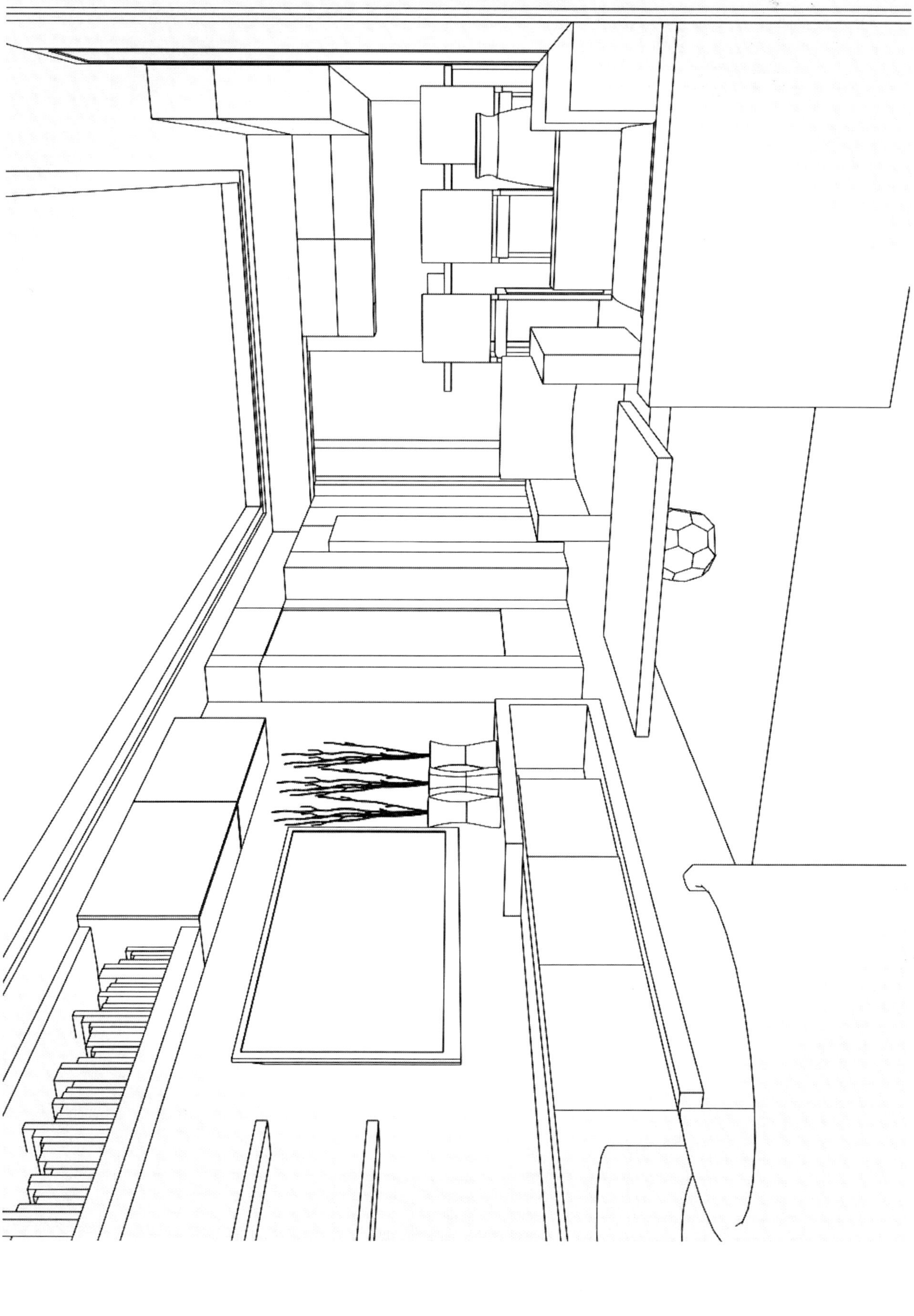

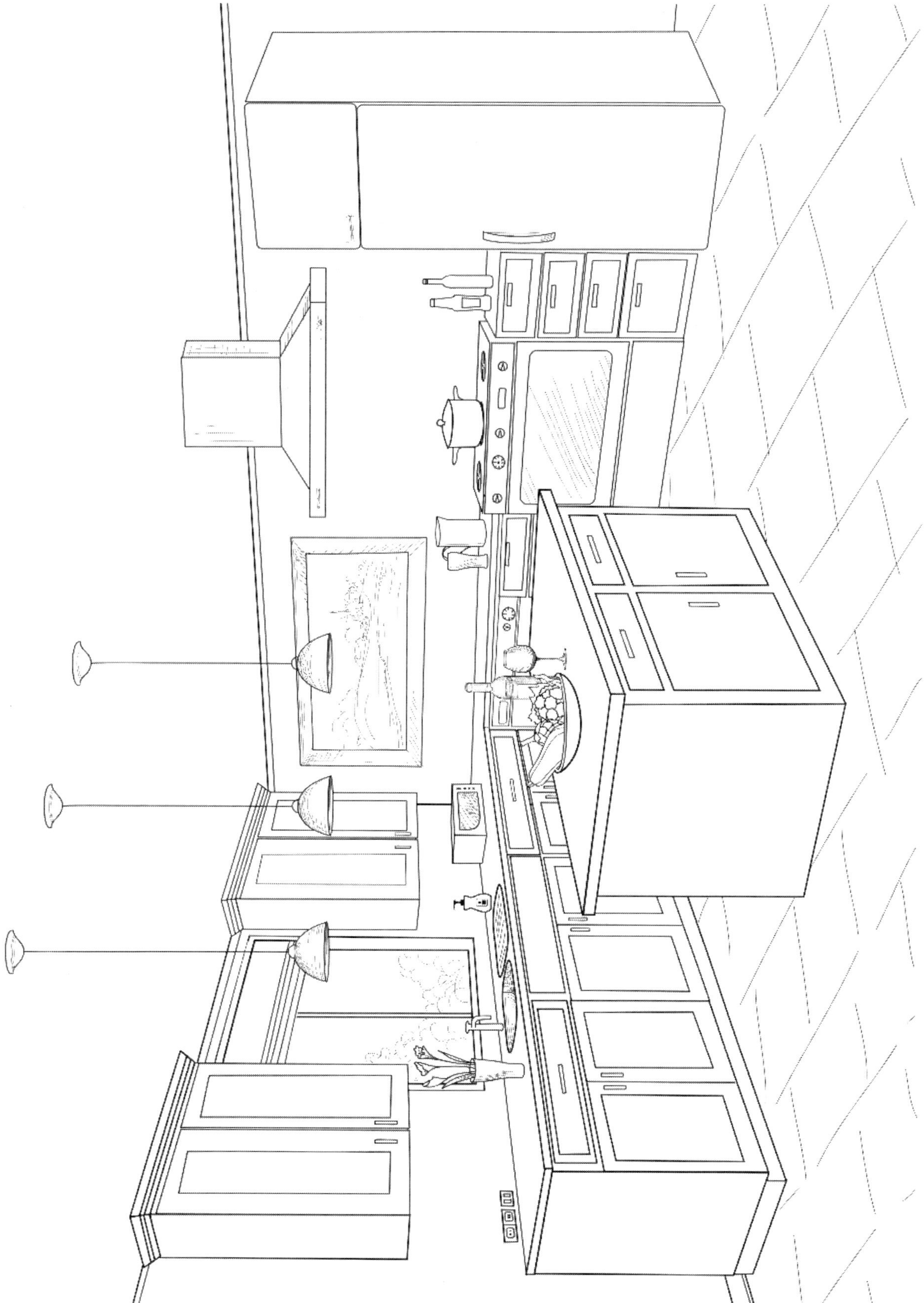

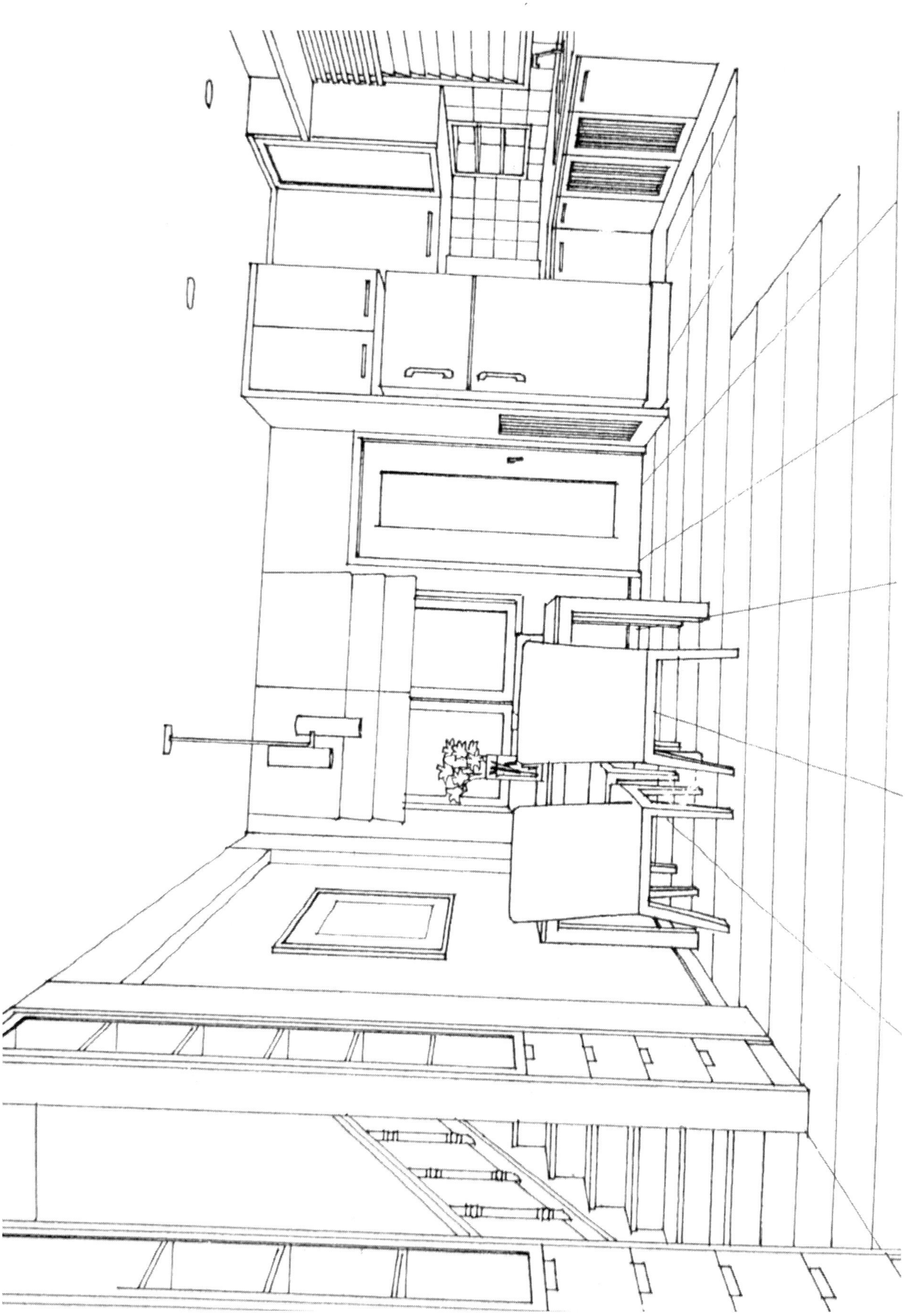

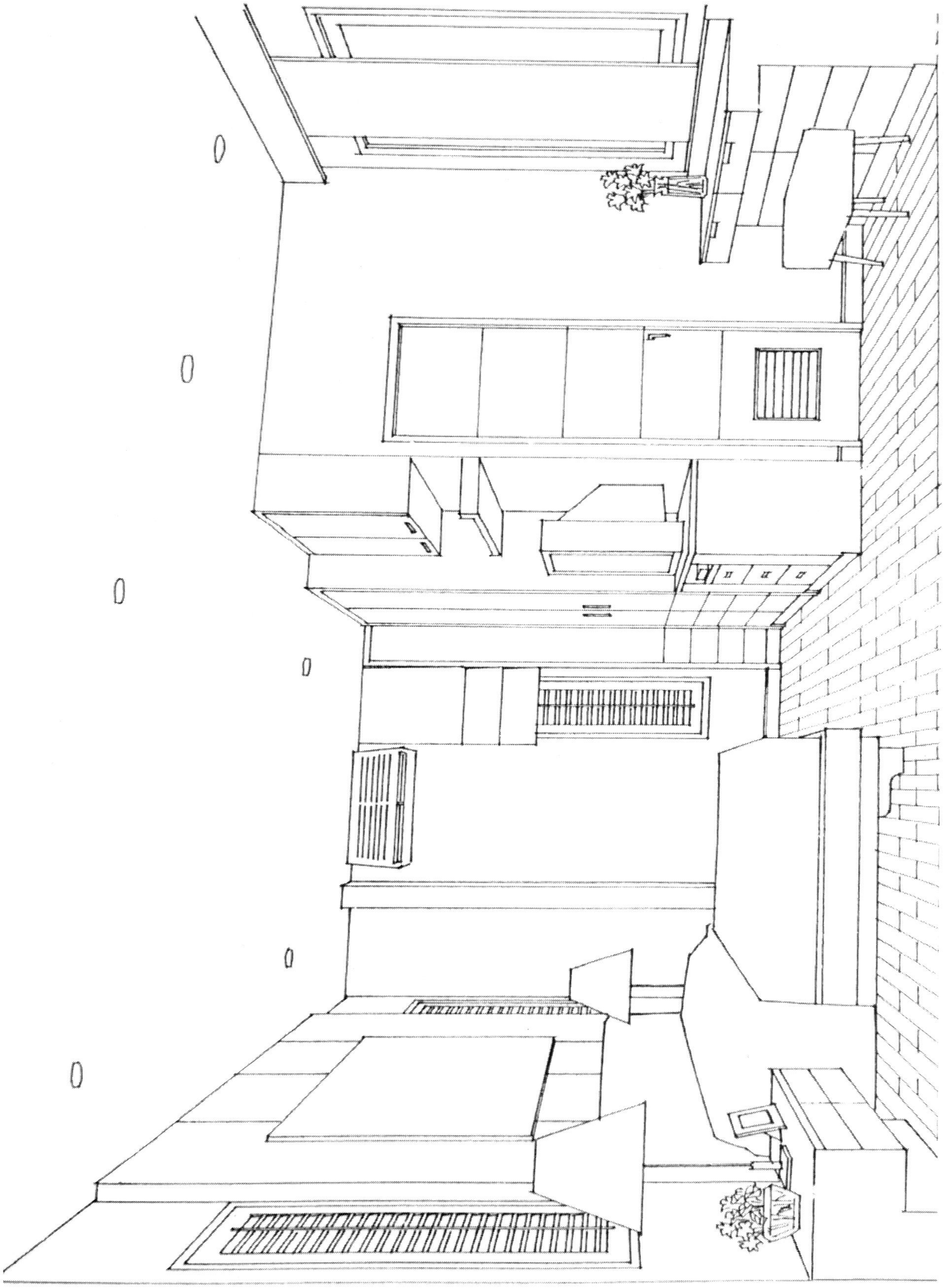

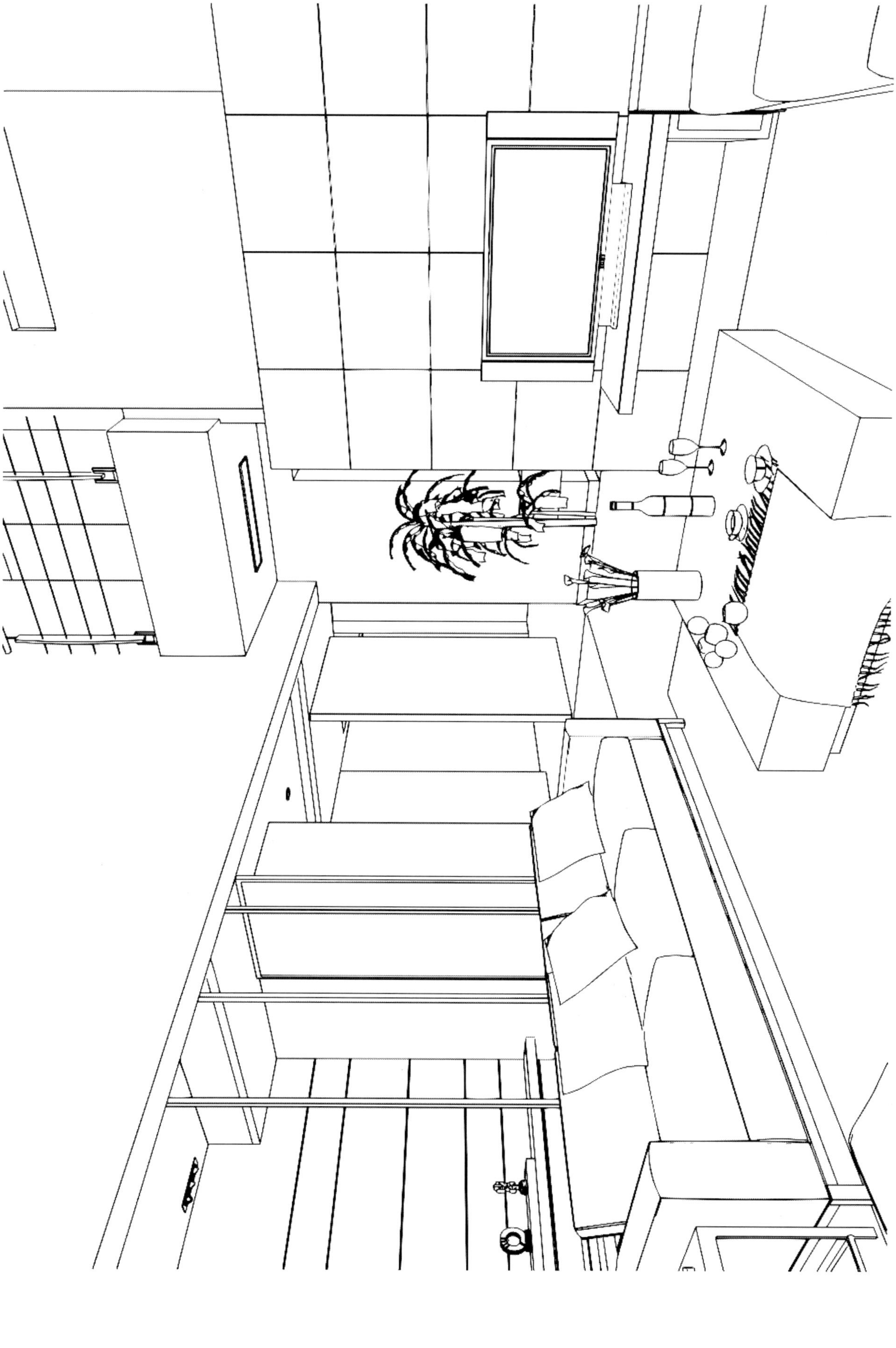

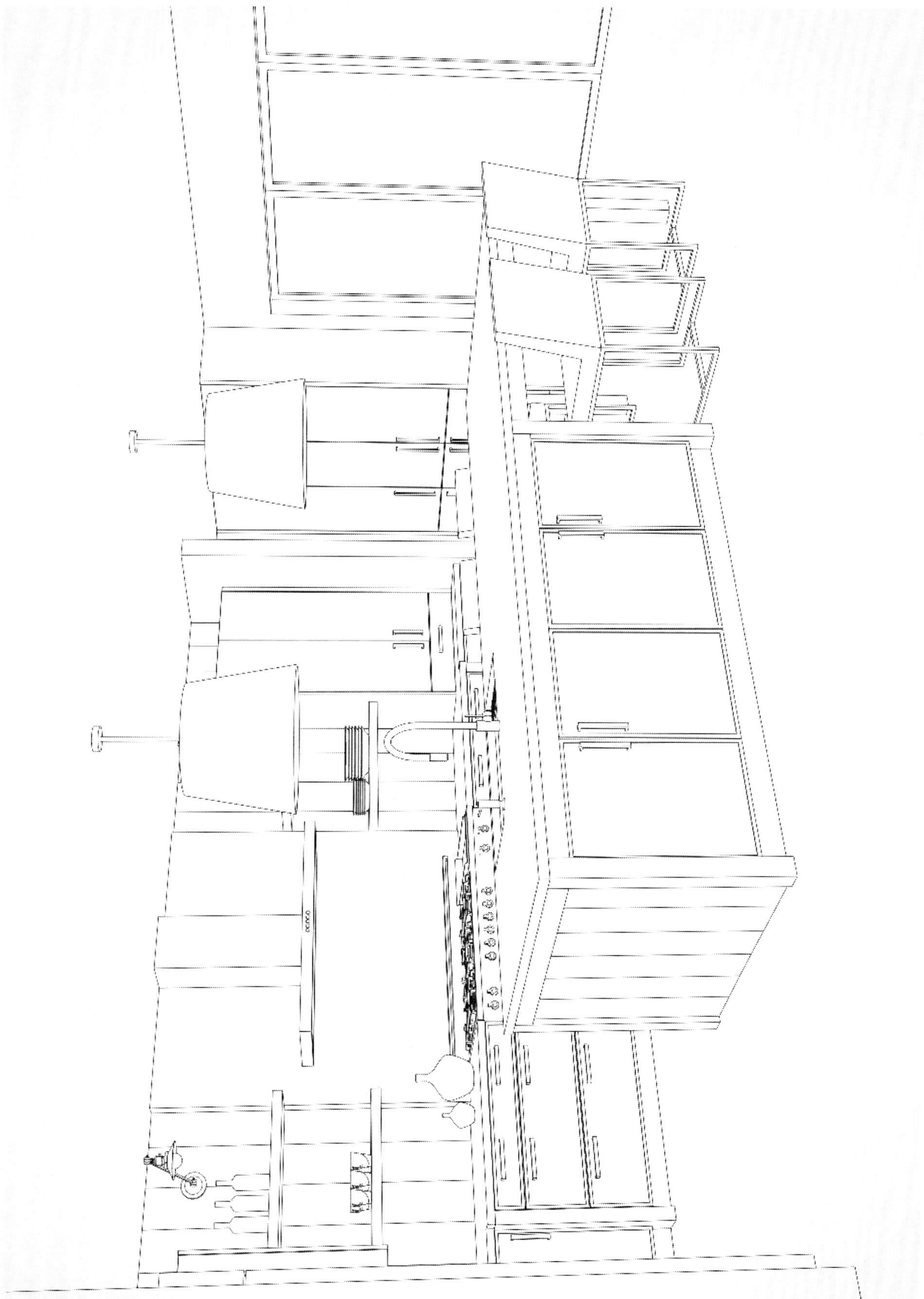

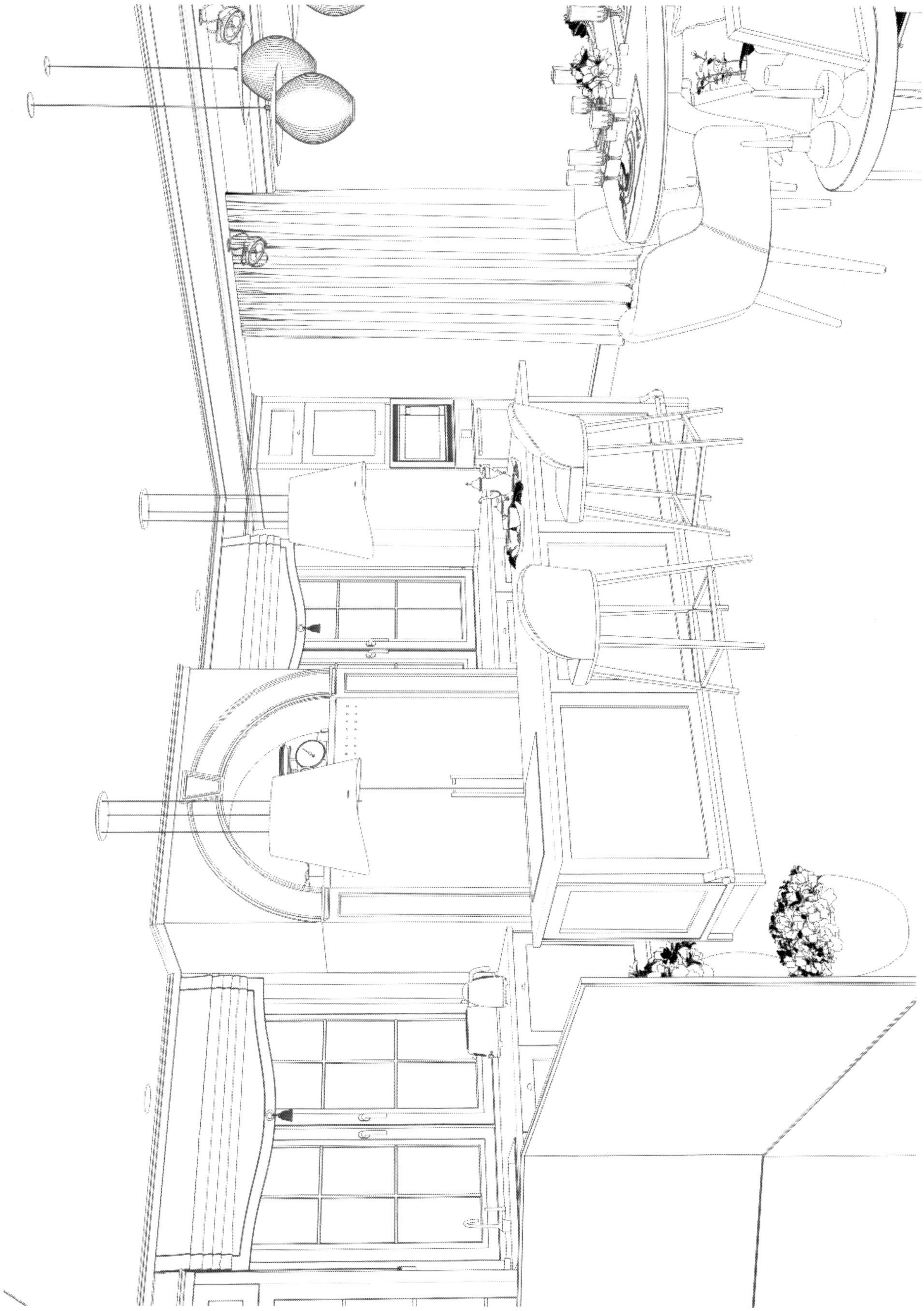

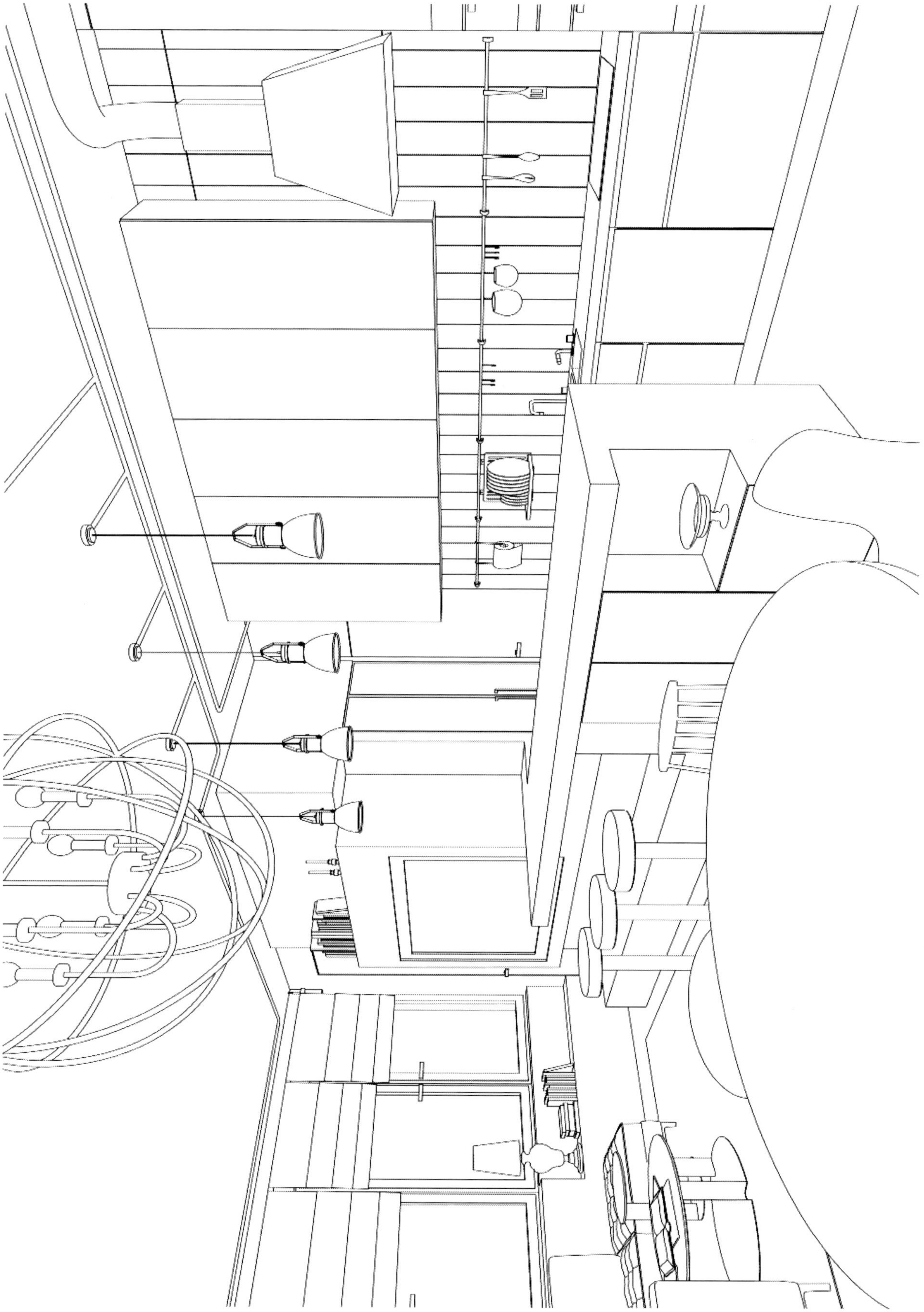

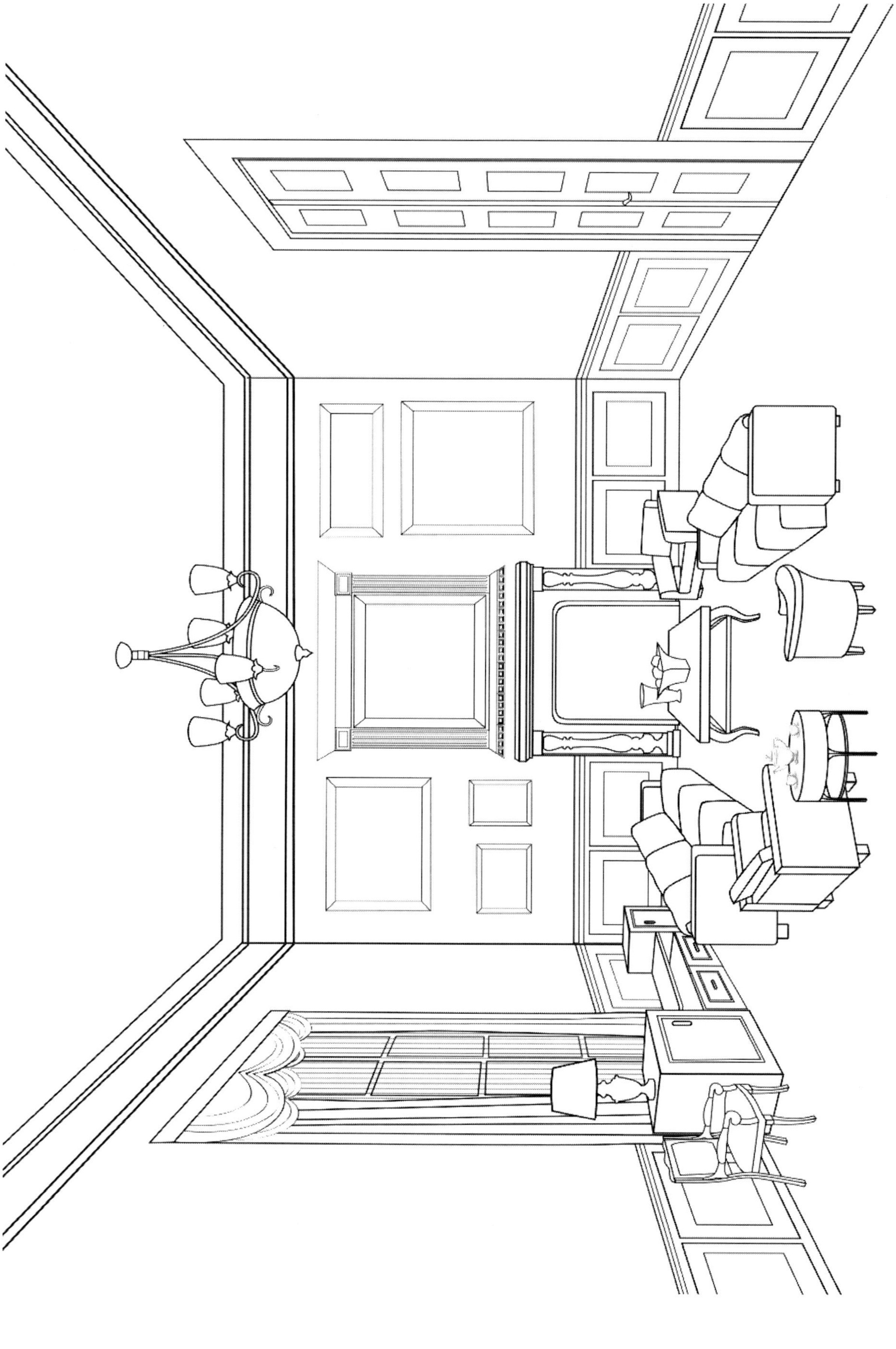

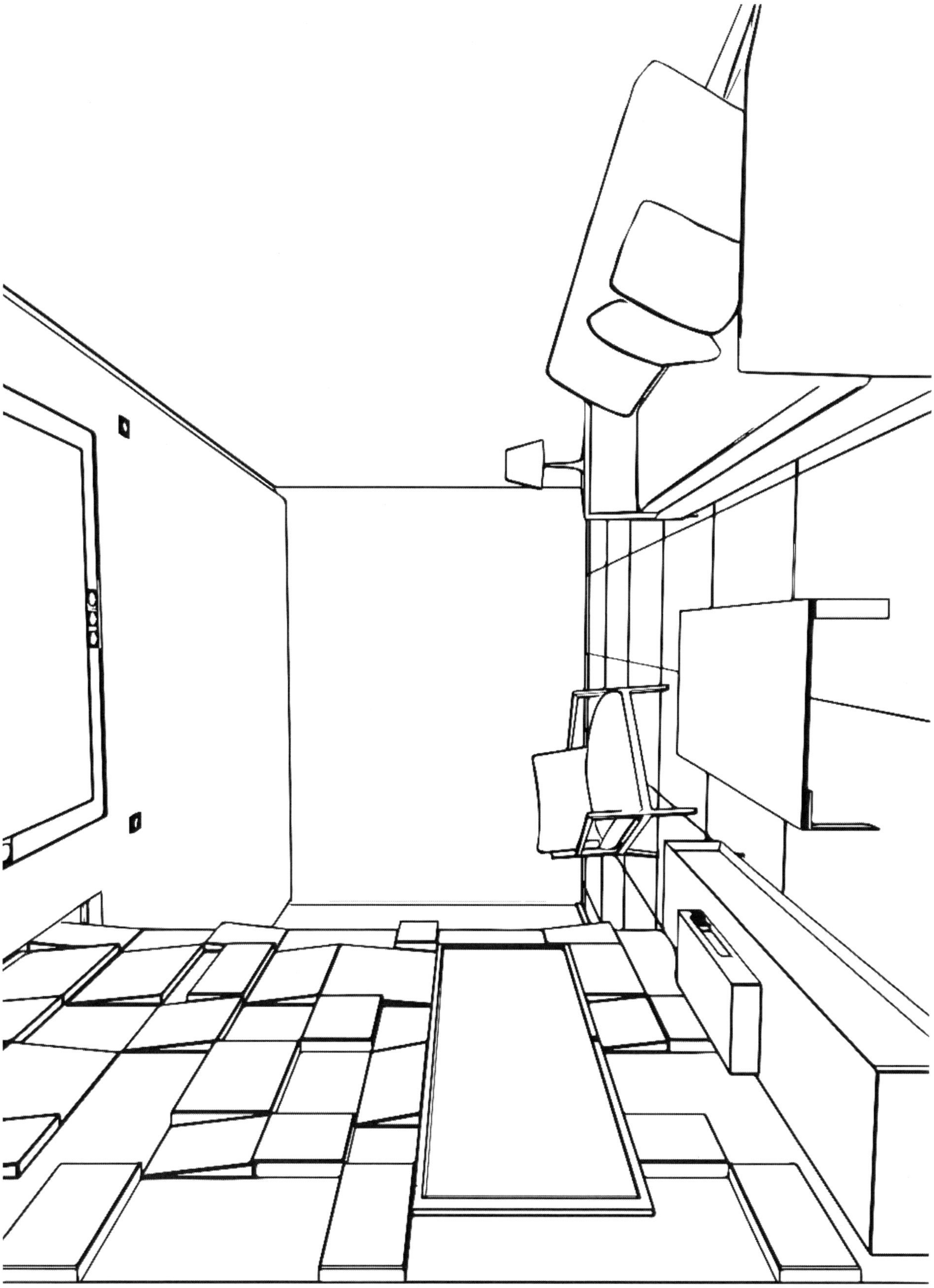

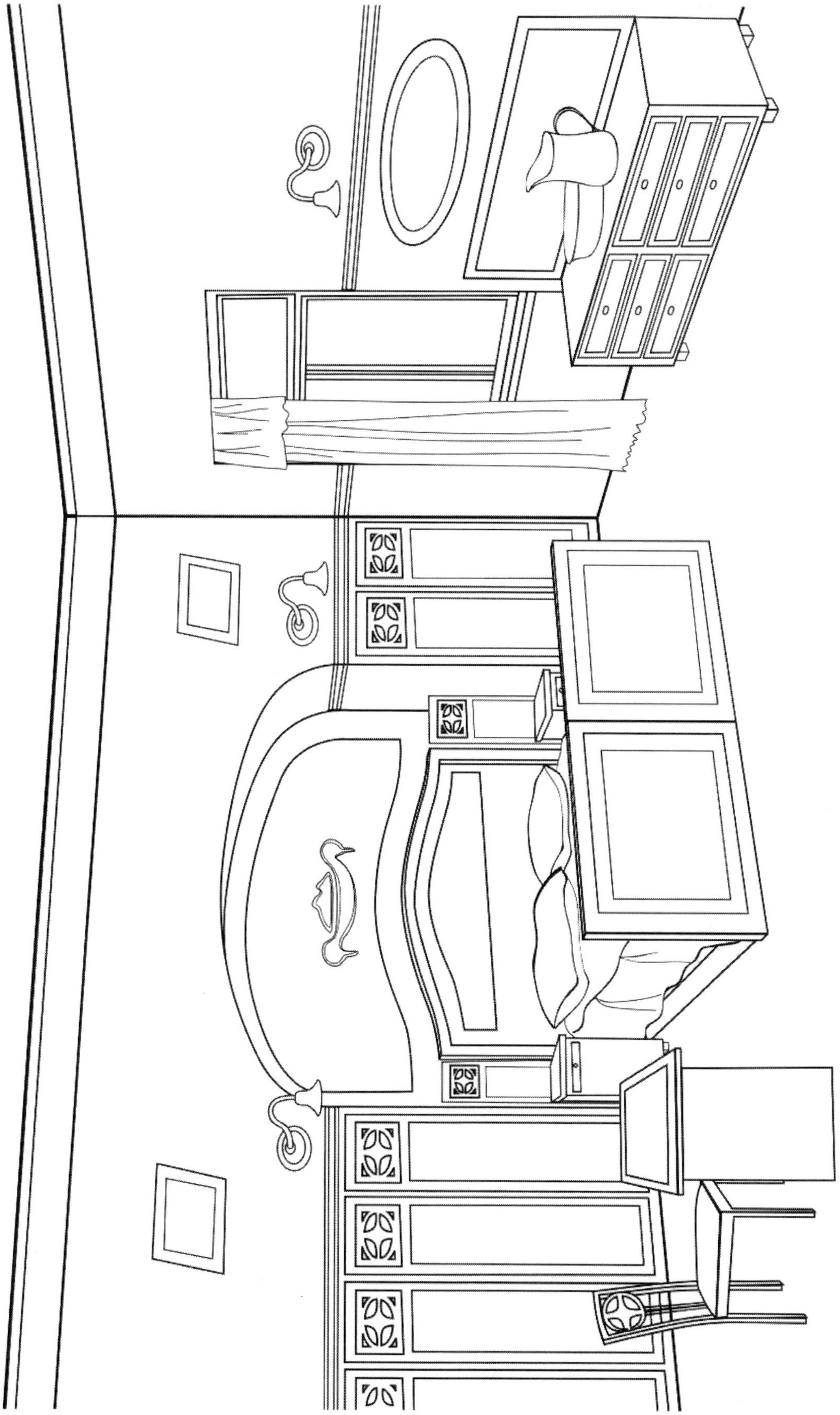

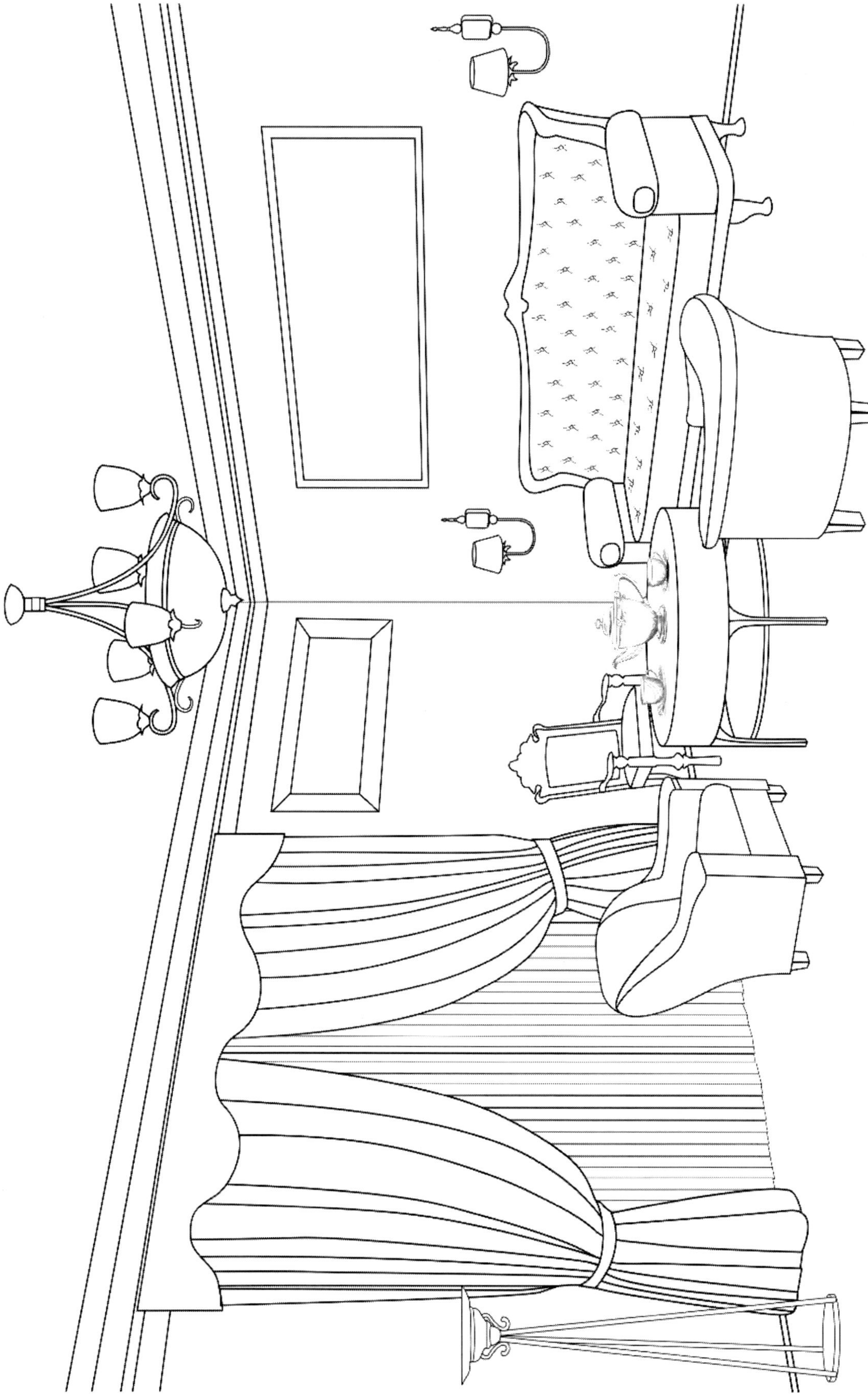

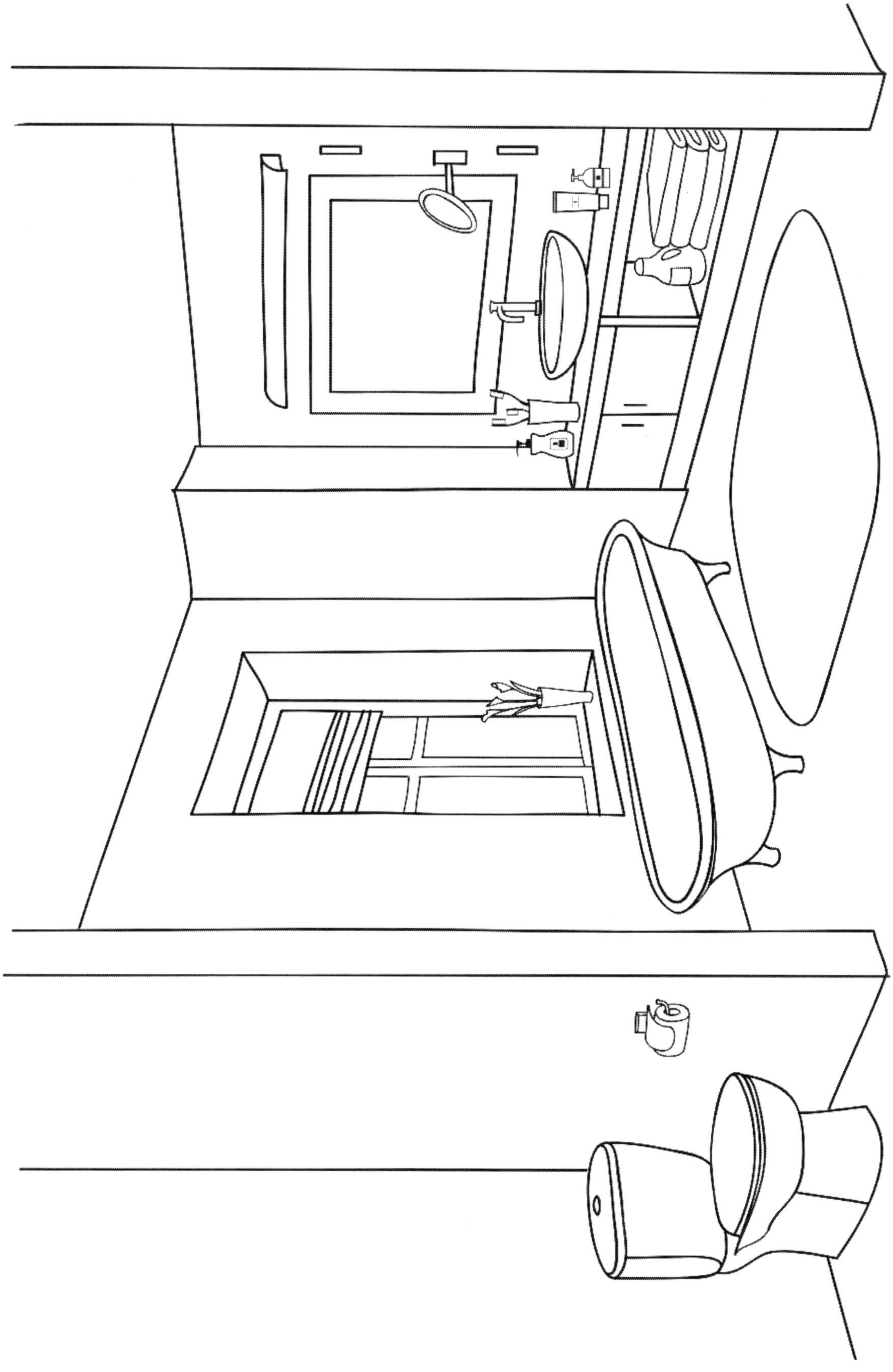

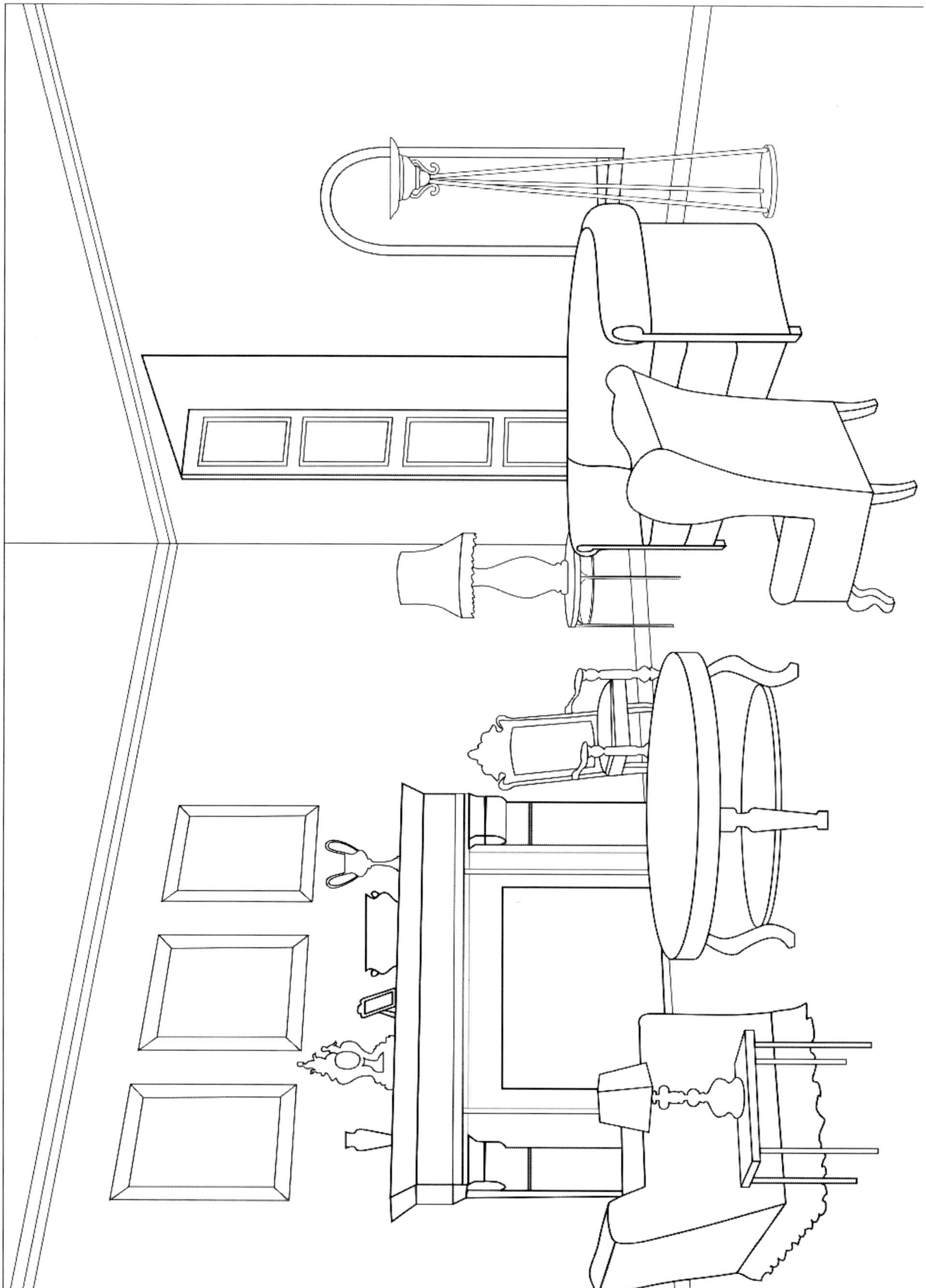

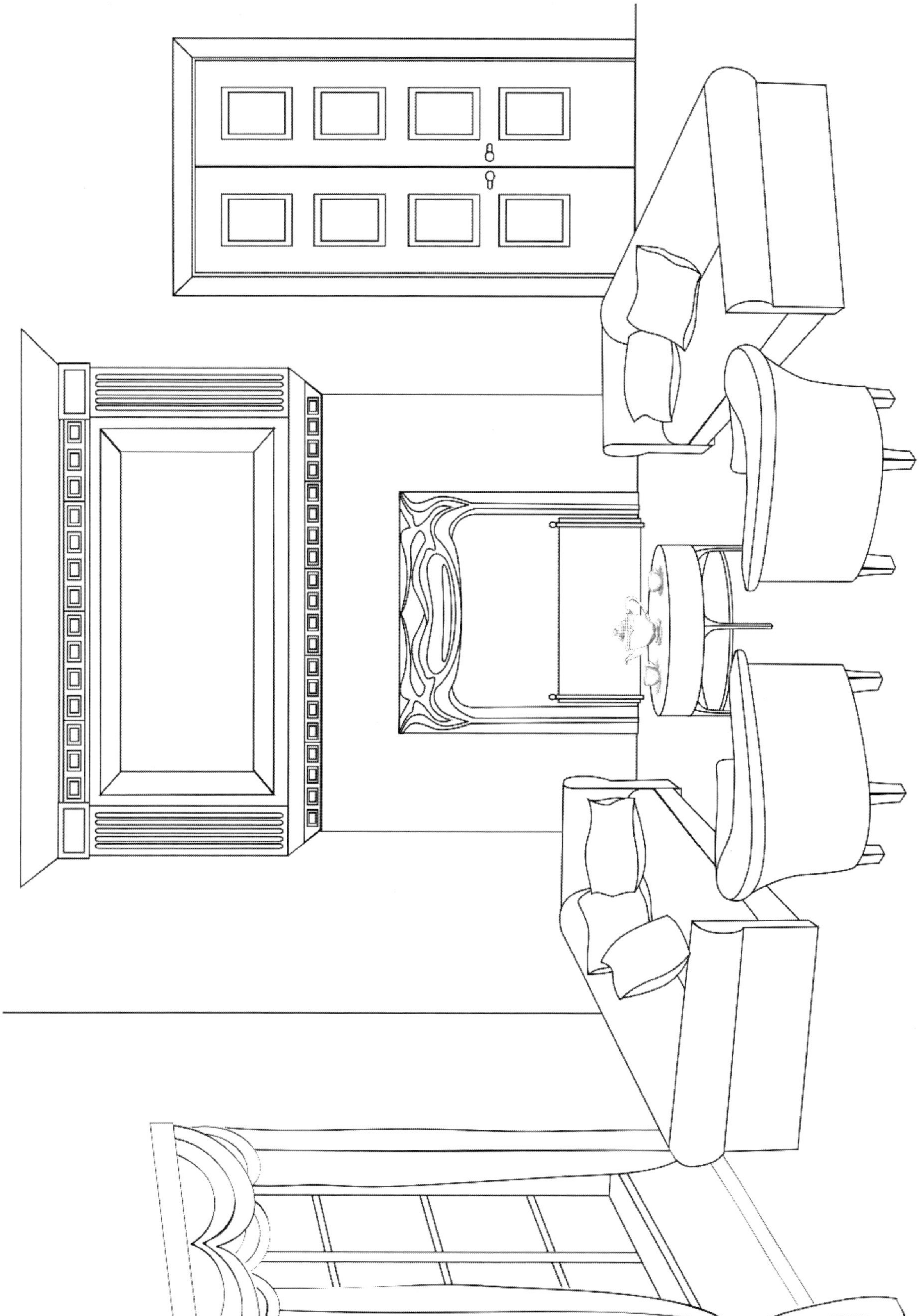

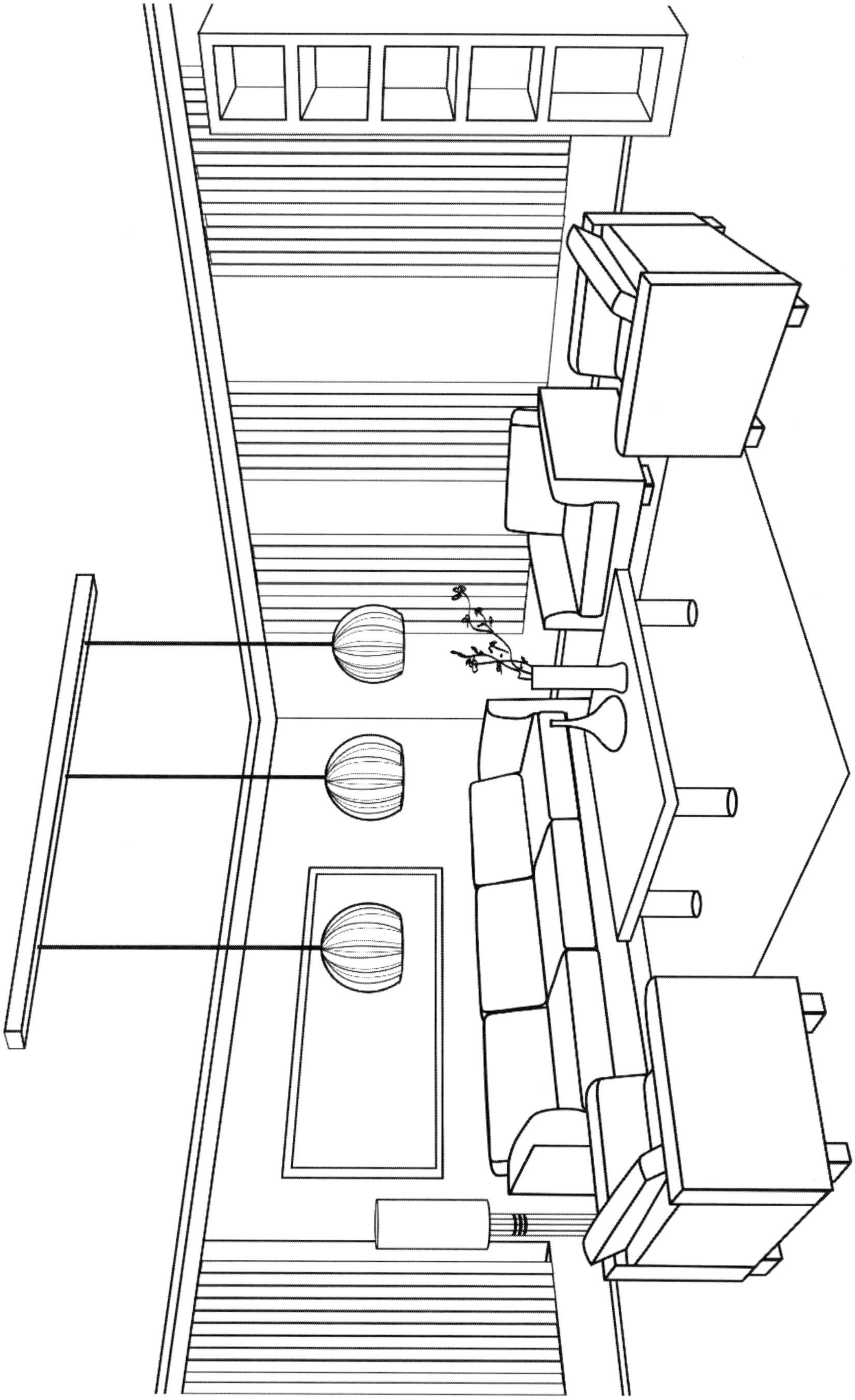

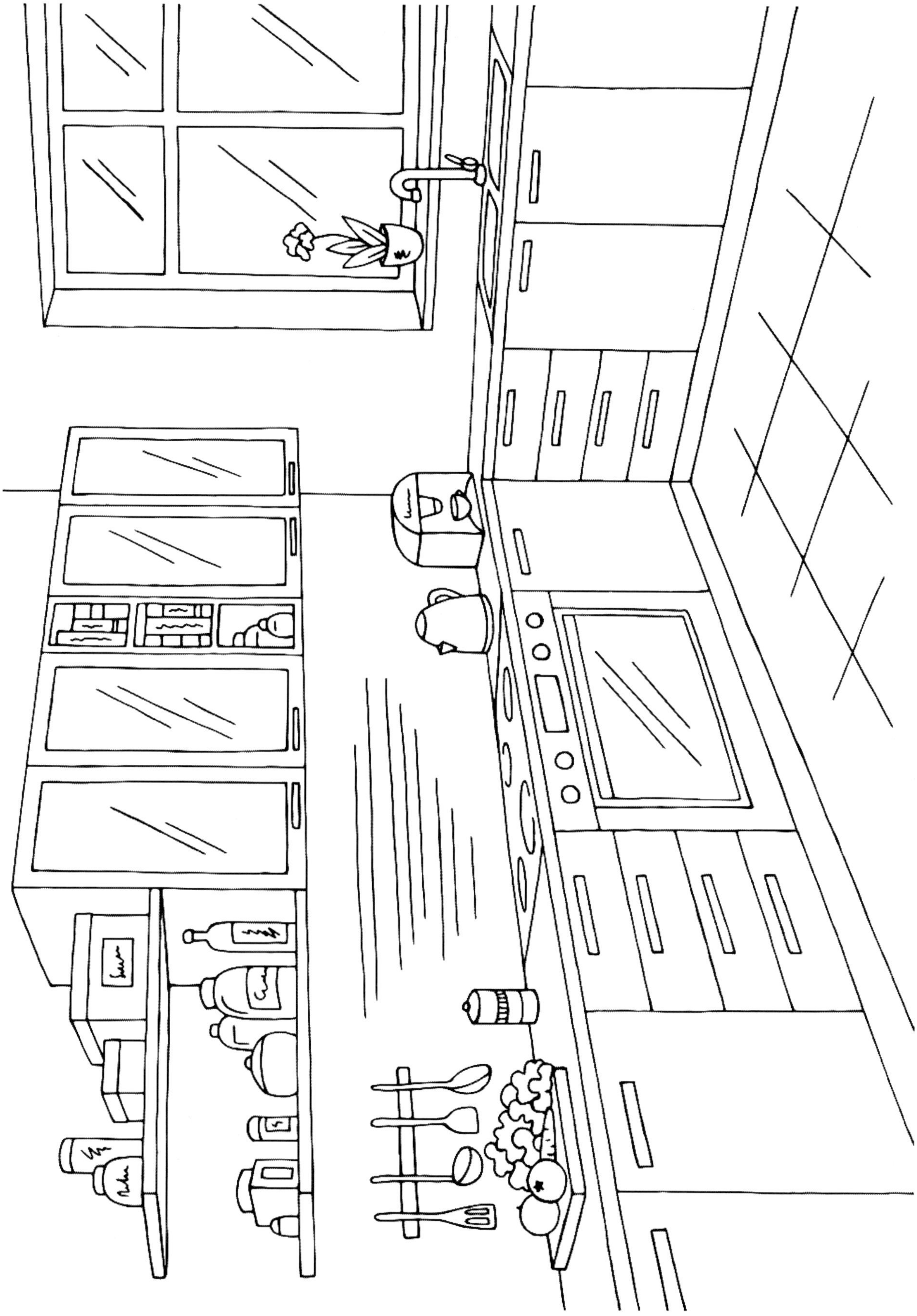

Made in United States
North Haven, CT
25 July 2022

21780944R00035